KU-579-053

Contents

Introduction

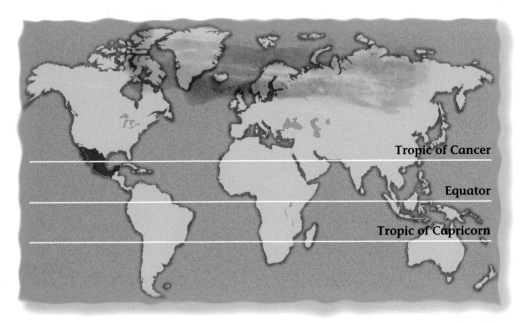

Tropic of Cancer

Equator

Tropic of Capricorn

Think of Mexico and maybe you think of chilli peppers, tortilla chips and sombreros. You might have heard of Acapulco or Cancun, where tourists bake on white sand beaches. Or perhaps you know something about the **Aztec** and the **Maya** Indians, who ruled Mexico long before Europeans even knew it was there. But there's more to Mexico than these few, familiar things.

△ **Where is Mexico?**

People and wealth

Eighty seven million people live in Mexico. The population has grown quickly, doubling in the last 20 years. Today half of all Mexicans are under fifteen years old. Most Mexicans are of part European and part Indian descent. Around 10 million are pure-blood Indians, and there are still some 50 different Indian peoples, like the Maya, the Nahua and the Zapotec.

Mexicans are proud of their Indian history, but Indians themselves are often among the poorest and most disadvantaged people in Mexico. Yet in some ways Mexico is a rich country. There are industries and oil refineries, car plants and textile factories. Mexico City, the country's capital, is one of the largest cities in the world – twice as big as London.

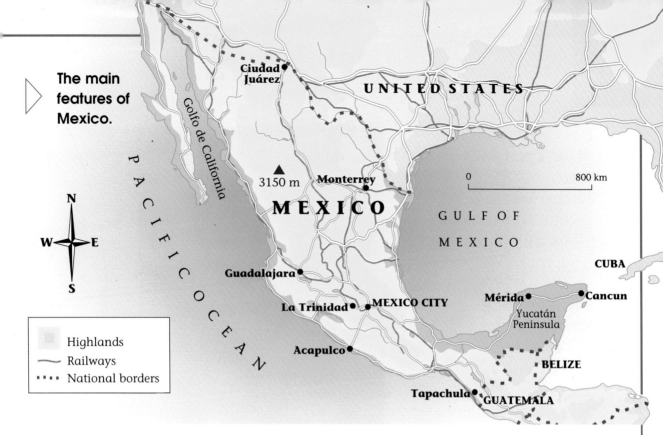

The main features of Mexico.

Legend:
- Highlands
- Railways
- National borders

Geography and climate

More than half of Mexico is 1000 metres or more above sea level. A high **plateau** runs roughly north to south through the centre of the country. To the north, it is low and dry, a semi-desert of cactus and scrub. In the south the land rises and becomes mountainous.

Thunderstorm clouds gather over volcanic mountains in southern Mexico.

The climate changes with altitude. On the flat coastal plains there is little rain, and it is hot – above 20° C all year. In the central highlands it is cooler and wetter – a **temperate** climate.

Half of Mexico is **arid**. There are often droughts, and only about a tenth of Mexico has rain all year round.

3

The people

Every year, on the Day of the Dead, Mexicans remember their **ancestors**. Families decorate graves and altars with flowers and food, and have parties.

The Maya and the Aztec

The ancestors that people celebrate on the Day of the Dead can be traced back to the original Indian peoples of Mexico. Two of the most powerful were the **Maya** and the **Aztec** who settled in the highlands of Mexico and Central America more than 1000 years ago. They were warrior peoples, but they also traded and farmed and built great cities, the ruins of which can still be seen today.

Europeans arrive

About 500 hundred years ago, just after Columbus sailed to the Americas, Spanish soldiers led by Hernán Cortés began the conquest of Mexico. In three years, between 1519 and 1521, they destroyed the Aztec empire, claiming Mexico as a Spanish **colony**. They took the Indians as slaves, and ruined most of their pyramids and cities. Millions of Indians died, either killed by soldiers, or by diseases introduced to the area by the Europeans.

△ Knowing how to farm and cook maize allowed the Aztec and Maya to flourish.

Spanish culture and civil war

It was the beginning of 300 years of rule from Spain. Spanish **culture** spread. Priests came and converted the Indians to Catholicism. New cities were built in the Spanish style with a **plaza** at their centre and a Catholic church. Spanish became the national language.

After independence was won from Spain in 1810, Mexico descended into 100 years of turmoil and war and lost almost half its territory (including Texas) to the USA.

△ This woman is from El Tejocote in the state of Queretaro.

The Mexican Revolution

By 1917 many ordinary Mexicans united in a **revolution**. They fought for the right to rule themselves, and to create a country where they could own their own land and in which there would be health care and education for all. This was the Mexican Revolution, and it was the birth of modern Mexico with its 31 states and **constitution**.

▽ Chocolate skulls go on sale for the Day of the Dead.

Many Mexicans feel the ideals people fought for then have been betrayed, and today the majority of Mexicans are poor. But life is not always grim. There are many **fiestas** or parties. At least once a year whole villages or towns will join in, dressing up, dancing, eating and drinking.

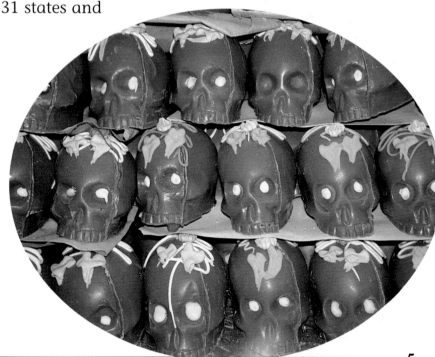

Where do people live?

Thirty years ago most Mexicans lived in the countryside. Now three-quarters of the population live in cities like Mexico City, Guadalajara and Monterrey.

City life

More than 20 million people live in Mexico City, a vast, bustling place. The centre is smart and modern. There are buses and an underground metro. Brightly painted taxis hurtle along the wide boulevards, among office blocks, pleasant houses and expensive shops.

But take a bus a few miles along one of the main motorways and you arrive in the slums. Millions of people live here. The roads are dirt tracks which turn to mud when it rains. Houses have one or two rooms, and are often built with old bits of corrugated iron, wood and plastic. Living is cramped and unhealthy. If there is running water it comes from a shared outside tap.

▽ **This is Mexico City. In the distance you can see volcanoes.**

△ Most people live in small, cheaply built houses.

Life in the countryside

The rainfall and soil needed for successful farming are best in Mexico's central highlands. Many Mexicans live here. Many other regions are sparsely populated, such as the north, which is **arid**, and the plains and scrubland of the Yucatán.

Most Mexicans who live in the countryside farm pieces of land not much bigger than one or two football pitches. Some people own or rent land, but since the **revolution** millions of families live on communal land. This is land everyone in a community agrees to use together. Selling communal land was once unthinkable. But now the government is trying to change agriculture and the laws protecting this land have been altered. Some of it is being sold to companies which grow **cash crops** for **export**. Once the land is sold, people have no way to feed themselves, and have to work on the new farms, or leave to find work in one of the big cities.

Agriculture

Good farmland is scarce in Mexico. Some of the land is too **arid** for crops. Other land is difficult to farm because it covers mountains and steep slopes. In some areas, such as the Yucatán, the soils are too thin to farm. **Soil erosion** is also a huge problem. Once the soil erodes, growing crops becomes more difficult than ever. But people have no other means of supporting themselves, and so they farm it anyway.

Land

What land there is is shared out unfairly, and there has often been fighting over who owns it. This was one of the causes of the 1917 **revolution**. By law, privately owned land must be divided between children when the parents die.

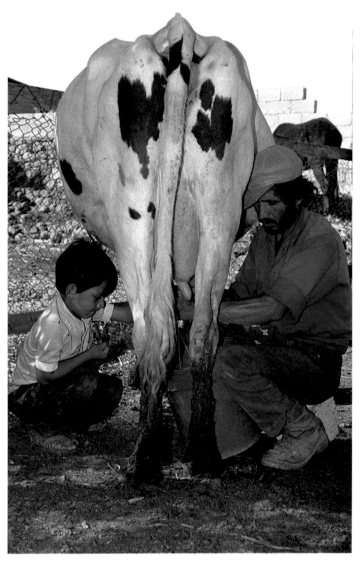

△ Many farmers keep a few animals.

Consequently farm sizes have become smaller over the generations as land is divided.

Sometimes the family of one brother or sister will keep the land, while the others leave to work in the cities. The farming family will eat what they grow, which is mostly maize and beans. What is left over will be sold at the local market, and they will spend the money on essentials like soap, sugar and cooking oil. These families are known as **subsistence farmers**. Sometimes they will grow a **cash crop** like coffee for money.

Big farms and imports

The wealthier farmers and companies have a lot of good land. Where there isn't enough rain, they can afford to use **irrigation**. They use machinery and grow many different crops for **export,** such as cotton, coffee and fruit. Raising cattle for beef is also important, especially in the dry north of Mexico.

However, as more export crops are grown and use up farmland, more food must be **imported** from abroad. Many Mexicans could afford to eat more healthily when Mexico grew all its own maize and beans.

Maize

Maize is Mexico's most important crop. Maize is a staple food – just as bread, potatoes or rice are for us. Everyone eats it and it has been grown there for 7000 years. Often it is ground, and the flour used to make 'tortillas' – flat maize pancakes. We even eat them here – cut into quarters, then fried and sold as tortilla chips.

▽ Not all farmers can afford machinery so land is often ploughed using horses.

Industry

Mexico has a rich economy. There are modern industries and plentiful **raw materials**.

△ A young dancer in an Aztec-style costume earns money from tourists.

Tourism and modern industry

Tourism is one of Mexico's biggest industries. More than 6 million holidaymakers visit every year, spending millions of pounds in hotels, restaurants and beach resorts like Acapulco. They come mainly for the sun, but also to visit the temples and pyramids that remain from the **Aztec** and **Maya** empires.

Most of Mexico's modern industry is in Mexico City, Guadalajara and Monterrey, and in a 20-kilometre wide strip along the border with the USA. Here there are more than 2000 factories making cars, televisions and computers for **export** to the USA.

Mexico uses iron ore to make steel. It uses cotton to make textiles. It has oil and makes chemicals. The land is also rich in minerals such as silver, gold and copper. Mexico's most valuable exports are cars, machinery and chemicals.

△ Small-scale industries, like making breeze blocks, use simple, cheap technology.

Trade

A new trade deal, known as NAFTA, has been signed between Mexico, the USA and Canada. The plan is that more trade will create more money and jobs for Mexico. But groups which represent farmers and poor people fear that the companies which come to Mexico may simply take advantage, treat workers badly, and pollute the environment. Another concern is that US government **subsidies** to American maize farmers will mean that Mexico will **import** US maize instead of buying from Mexican peasant farmers. Wages are already very low in Mexico (about £2 a day).

Making a living

Many Mexicans have little to do with modern industry. They work for themselves as street traders selling clothes, tortillas, beans and hot snacks and crafts. Gloria Bautista's son is ten years old. He goes out to collect rubbish to sell for recycling. He may only bring home five to seven pesos (about a pound), but he uses that to buy his things for school.

The rich and the poor

Lots of children in Mexico have to work to earn money for their families.

Mexico, as we have seen, is a rich country. It has oil and industry. It makes cars and computers. However, this wealth is not shared equally among its people. The 35 richest families in Mexico have as much wealth between them as the 15 million poorest people.

Poverty and debt

More than half of all Mexicans are very poor. They die sooner, earn less and eat less than rich Mexicans. They live in bad housing and are lucky if they can afford hospitals or schools.

This startling difference between the way people live in Mexico is the country's biggest challenge. Unfortunately in the last few years this difference has increased.

Part of the problem is that Mexico borrowed billions of dollars to build new industries. Now it has to pay the money back, and there is not enough left over for schools and hospitals. 'There are many economic problems,' says Eliazar Nieto from the village of La Trinidad. 'Everything changes quickly: the price of petrol and food is always rising and we don't know what to do from one day to the next.'

The southern state of Chiapas, is one of the poorest states. Here Indian farmers are fighting the army and gunmen hired by the big landowners, for land the Indians believe is rightfully theirs.

Emigration and families
In the north of Mexico thousands of Mexicans cross the border into the USA. Some **emigrate** legally, but many can't get **work visas** so have to climb the border fences and make a run for it during the night. Even the worst jobs in the USA will pay more than work they can get in Mexico.

Many of those who do have jobs still find life hard.

The only way people survive is by relying on each other. In families, everybody from cousins to grandparents, will help each other. Those with a job, or who emigrate to the USA, help support family and relatives back home.

If you have money, there is everything you could want in Mexico.

La Trinidad

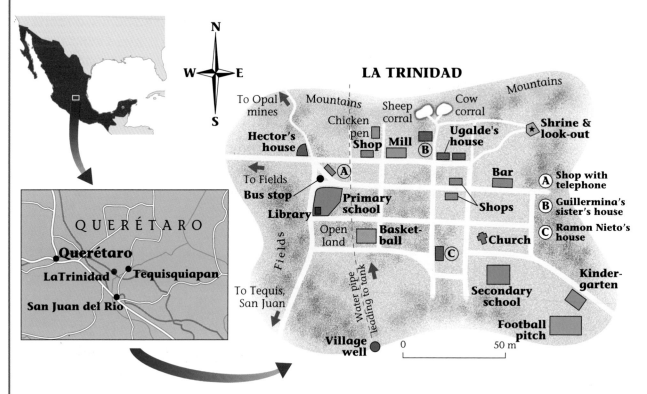

The village of La Trinidad.

La Trinidad is a village in the state of Querétaro in central Mexico. There are some small shops, a church, a public telephone, a library, and a mill where the women go to grind maize. The land around is fertile, part of a wide valley that slopes down to the San Juan River. In summer the valley is hot and dry and, up behind the village, cacti grow on the rocky cliffs.

A dusty road leads out of La Trinidad to the nearest town, Tequisquiapan, or 'Tequis' for short, eleven kilometres away.

Homes and families

About 2000 people live in La Trinidad. The houses are small and built of stone or breeze blocks with roofs of tiles and grey asbestos sheeting.

The Ugalde family live in La Trinidad. They are Juan and Guillermina, and their seven children, aged between seven and seventeen. Their house has three rooms; one is a kitchen and living room, and the other two are bedrooms.

The children share one bedroom, sleeping head-to-toe in two double beds. The family also has a bathroom, a store room and a garden for flowers, vegetables, tomatoes and chilli peppers.

Water, electricity and roads

La Trinidad, like many villages in Mexico, is changing quickly. Organized by their village council, the people of La Trinidad have laid cobbled streets where there used to be only dirt tracks. They've persuaded the government to put in mains electricity, so most houses now have fridges, televisions and electric light.

Villagers also persuaded the federal government to help them build a water and sewerage system. Now there are flush toilets, and piped water from a deep well bored below the village. It's a lot easier than carrying water in buckets from the old well.

△ Mrs Ugalde with three of her children.

▷ Juan Ugalde looks out over La Trinidad.

Village life

La Trinidad is a farming community. Nearly every family in the village owns a few acres of land.

Farming and animals

Juan Ugalde is a farmer. From April he's busy in the fields, ploughing and planting the seeds, which he saved from the previous year's harvest. Juan still uses horses for ploughing, though some farmers hire tractors.

There's no **irrigation** in La Trinidad so everyone makes the most of the rain. Planting begins with the rainy season in May. Juan grows maize and beans – not to sell, but for the family to eat. He usually harvests enough to last the year, and stores it in the village.

▽ Juan and his son Manuel groom their horses and donkey.

△ Hector Montes cuts, polishes and sells opals found in the mines.

Juan's neighbour, Martin Nieto, keeps eleven dairy cows. The cows were expensive and Martin had to borrow from a savings club to buy them. He earns enough selling the milk to keep his family going, though he still has a lot of debt. Most families keep some smaller animals – chickens, sheep or pigs. They're not so expensive to buy and are easier to look after.

Earning a living

As well as farming most people have to do another job just to make a living. When Juan Ugalde isn't farming he supports his family by labouring on building sites around the village. When there's no labouring work he goes to the **opal** mines.

The mines are a series of caves and rock faces, an hour's walk from La Trinidad. Anyone is free to try their luck, but the work is hard and boring. Often, after a long day spent cracking rocks looking for the small white opals, Juan will still come home empty-handed. At weekends his sons sometimes help him.

School

In Mexico schooling is free, though parents have to pay for some of the books needed for lessons and the school uniform. Nearly all children go at least to primary school because everyone feels it's important. Juan Ugalde says 'My dream is for the children to go to school and learn well, or they will have no future.'

Today more Mexican children have the opportunity to learn than in the past. In Juan's childhood fewer than one in ten children in the village could read or write. But even now teenagers often drop out of school because their families need the money they can earn.

▽ Rosio's sister, seven-year-old Marisol enjoys school.

Schools in La Trinidad

In La Trinidad there are three schools: a kindergarten for under-fives, a primary school for six to twelve-year-olds and the secondary school. The school buildings are modern, and there are sports fields and playgrounds.

School starts at 8 a.m., and finishes at 12.30 p.m., or 2 p.m. in the secondary school.

△ Rosio Ugalde at the secondary school with her friends.

◁ Marisol and Miguel-Angel Ugalde set off for school with their cousin.

Lessons

The primary school has 230 pupils spread among six classes. Here Marisol Ugalde learns to read and write, and studies Spanish, history, maths, science, art and PE.

Lessons at the secondary school begin with fifteen minutes of educational television, beamed in via a satellite dish on the roof. The broadcasts cover the national curriculum for schools all over Mexico.

There are three classes in the secondary school and most students are aged between twelve and fifteen. The subjects would all be familiar to students in the UK, except with Spanish instead of English. But the school also has a vegetable garden, and students study agriculture.

If young people want to go to college they must pay to travel to the towns of Tequis or San Juan to study. Very few ever do because it is too expensive for most families.

Spare time

Men sit and talk and play dominoes.

Spare time for young people like the Ugalde children, is often spent helping out – with the animals, around the house, or looking for **opals** with their father.

There are always chores to do – but is it just work? For Manuel Ugalde who rides the donkey to the stream to drink, or for his brother who herds the sheep, it is hard to say whether it's work or play.

Sport

When it comes to sport, football and basketball are the favourites of the village and the whole of Mexico. La Trinidad has one of the best football teams in the area, and there are matches against other village teams on Saturdays. In the cool of the evenings Rosio Ugalde plays basketball with her friends on concrete courts in the village.

The Church

The Catholic Church is very important to Mexicans. On Sundays the whole family puts on their best clothes for mass at the local church. On Saturdays younger children go to **catechism** class, led by teenagers from La Trinidad.

Television has become very much a part of Mexican life. Soap operas, or 'novelas', have millions of devoted viewers. Most of the other television programmes are imported from the USA, and dubbed into Spanish.

The Ugalde children read comics or 'photo-novelas' – romance or adventure stories which have real photos set out like comic strips.

In large towns like Tequis, or San Juan, there are different things to do – and better facilities. Roller-bladers and cyclists whizz around the smooth pavements and squares. There are video arcades, parks, swimming pools, cinemas and bookshops.

▽ **Edgar Ugalde and his cousin herd sheep to pasture. It's work but it can be fun as well.**

A day with the Ugalde family

▽ **Guillermina makes tortillas every day.**

Guillermina Ugalde has ten brothers and sisters, all living nearby, and Juan has eight. Their brothers and sisters also have children, so the Ugaldes' children have many aunts, uncles and cousins to visit or stay with.

Manuel Ugalde, aged nine, usually lives with his aunt. His brother, sixteen-year-old Adrian, sleeps at his grandmother's next door.

Morning

The family gets up at 6 a.m. Guillermina is first up. She cooks breakfast. There are scrambled eggs and beans on the stove, tortillas roasting, and the smell of coffee and hot chocolate. Edgar feeds the budgie. Miguel-Angel gets the eggs from the hens in the garden. The kitchen is crowded and loud music is playing on the radio to wake everyone up.

By 7.50 a.m. the children have packed a mid-morning snack and set off to school. Then it's Juan's turn to have breakfast.

Guillermina carries a bucket of soaked maize to the mill two streets away. She waits with the other women to have her corn ground into a thick paste to make tortillas.

She roasts the tortillas at her sister's house. She makes a large pile – enough for the day and the following day's breakfast. Then it's home to wash the dishes at the tap in the yard. Later she hand-washes clothes and hangs them on the line to dry.

Afternoon

By 2 p.m. everyone is back home for the main meal of the day. Once or twice a week the Ugaldes eat chicken, and every day there are beans, tortillas, rice and tomatoes. Sometimes there are treats like 'chili rellenos', which are peppers stuffed with cheese.

△ Marisol does her homework in the afternoon.

The Ugaldes have twelve sheep, and in the afternoon Edgar takes them from the corral under the cliff to graze on the hillside. Marisol and Miguel-Angel do their homework. Manuel's special job is riding the family's donkey down to the stream to drink, and giving it hay.

◁ Breakfast time in the Ugalde household.

Everyone is home again by the evening, when the family sits down for a meal together. There are leftovers from lunch, and bread and warm milk.

Few people in La Trinidad can afford a car or a pick-up truck. To get to work they walk to their fields or to the **opal** mines. Most things people need are within walking distance. The shops, the clinic, the school and many of their relatives are all close by. Occasionally a travelling salesman, or a shoe repairer calls at the village.

Ramon Nieto has a pick-up truck. He sells milk around the village, and loads up **alfalfa** for animals. The truck is his livelihood.

Travelling beyond La Trinidad

To travel farther, to Tequis or San Juan, people take a taxi or the bus. From San Juan it's a two-hour bus ride to Mexico City. There's a train too, but it's slower. However it's not often that any of the villagers can afford or need to go that far.

▽ Villagers from La Trinidad travel to the bustling daily market in Tequis.

Only the younger villagers travel a lot. They go to work in the factories in the industrial town of San Juan about 20 kilometres away. Sometimes they go even farther, north to the USA. Leopoldo is 29. Every year he works for nine months on the big farms in California. 'I prefer to work in the USA,' says Leopoldo. 'I can earn much more money to send home to my family. But it's getting more difficult to cross the border.'

△ A street trader makes a living selling pots in Tequis.

Tequis

Tequis is the place people from La Trinidad most often visit. There's a daily market with stalls selling everything from kitchen utensils to radios and cassettes, seeds and fertilizer, fruit and wine. There are also chemists and a hospital. Several buses go each day and the round trip costs about 20 pence.

At weekends Tequis' central square comes alive. Sometimes on Sundays there is an open-air mass in front of the cathedral. Hundreds of people gather for the service. Afterwards dancers perform in fantastic **Aztec** costumes for the tourists. On the other side of the square a brass band blasts away, while townspeople and tourists mingle and relax.

Journeys

Going by bus

Most Mexicans travel by bus. Buses are cheap and they go everywhere. On the long-distance routes you can travel first-class in gleaming buses with air conditioning and toilets. If you don't have much money you go third-class. It's slower and less comfortable but you still get to where you want to go. Distances are vast, and journeys from Mexico City to Mérida in the Yucatán, or to Tapachula in Chiapas, will take more than 24 hours.

Even small towns have their own bus station, or street or square, called 'la central', where the buses pull in and out. These are favourite places for food sellers and you can buy tortillas, roasted maize or beans, to keep you going on your journey.

In the countryside many of the roads are only dirt or gravel and so they are very bumpy. Buses here are old, and they rattle and shake with their cargoes of farmers and families travelling to market, or to see relatives.

△ When there isn't a bus you can usually hitch a lift on a pick-up truck to finish your journey.

Donkeys, bicycles and the metro

Horses and donkeys are used to transport farm produce and firewood. This is slow but cheap, and it is also good for mountain tracks. Many people also walk long distances, carrying heavy loads.

On Mexico City's metro there's only one fare, wherever you go. More than 4 million travellers use the metro each day, and at rush hour the carriages are crammed. Up above ground buses, taxis and cars spew fumes into the thin mountain air. There are more than 3 million private cars, and many thousands of buses which cause snake-like traffic jams across the city.

▽ In Mexico City the metro underground railway is usually crowded with travellers.

Bikes and motor bikes are used widely, often loaded with as many people or as much luggage as possible. One motorbike might carry three or four people, or a bike a whole stack of newspapers almost three metres high.

Looking at Mexico

△ **A saint's day procession in Tequis.**

▽ **Enjoying a day out in Chapultapec Park, Mexico City.**

Mexico City is a reminder of just how different the whole country of Mexico can be. You see the old and the new. You can see Indian **culture** and Spanish-speaking culture mixing in languages, clothes and customs. Walk through Mexico City and you see huge contrasts. You can see the ruins of great Aztec pyramids beside modern high-rise buildings.

These differences make Mexico an exciting place to be. You can enjoy the food – the spicy flavours, the beans and the tortillas. You can see colourful processions and visit the markets and **fiestas**.

The challenge for the future

But as we have seen in this book, one of the most striking differences is between the lives of the rich and the poor.

Mexicans see these differences too. Many work very hard to try to ensure that everyone gets a chance to enjoy what's good about Mexico, not just a lucky few.

△ **Playing on the beach at Zihuatanejo on the Pacific coast.**

▽ **Soldiers on parade on the Zocalo, the central square in Mexico City.**

For example 'Super Barrio', a community leader dressed up as a comic book super hero, leads campaigns by poor people to get water or rubbish collection in the slums.

Mexicans face hard choices about how the country's wealth can be shared more equally, and how to provide a better future for the young people that make up over half the population.

Glossary

Alfalfa A green, leafy plant used for animal feed.

Ancestors The people from whom you are descended – your grandparents, their parents and grandparents before them, and so on.

Arid An arid climate is very dry with little rain.

Aztec The Aztec settled in central Mexico from about AD900. They began to build up a civilization and construct cities in the 1300s. They were constantly at war with neighbouring peoples and made many enemies. The Spanish used these enemies to help them defeat the Aztecs.

Cash crops Crops which are grown to be sold, rather than eaten.

Catechism A way of learning about a religion in a question-and-answer form.

Colony When settlers take over a country, and claim it as their own or for their own country they colonize it.

Constitution The set of basic laws by which a state is governed.

Culture A people's whole way of life. This includes their ideas, beliefs, language, values, knowledge, customs and the things they make.

Emigrate To move to, and settle in another country.

Exports Goods that are sold to, or traded with another country.

Fiesta A spanish word for a party or celebration.

Imports Goods brought in from another country.

Irrigation A way of providing water for plants with channels or pipes.

Maya One of the world's great civilizations. The Maya ruled several city states in southern Mexico. They were the first people in this part of the world to invent writing.

Opal A white, semi-precious stone used in jewellery making.

Plateau A high, flat area of land.

Plaza The Spanish word for town square.

Raw materials The basic materials, like cotton or iron ore, from which finished goods are made.

Revolution A change to government or the way a country is run, often achieved by force.

Soil erosion When soil is washed away by rain or wind. Farming makes this more likely by breaking up the soil and removing the trees or plants that helped to keep it in place.

Subsidy Government money given to keep down the price of products.

Subsistence farmers Farmers who produce only enough to support their households.

Temperate A temperate climate is one that is neither hot nor cold. The UK has a temperate climate.

Work visa Permission to work in another country.

Index

About Oxfam in Mexico

The international family of Oxfams works with poor people and their organizations in over 70 countries. Oxfam believes that all people have basic rights: to earn a living, and to have food, shelter, health care, and education. Oxfam provides relief in emergencies, and gives long-term support to people struggling to build a better life for themselves and their families.

Oxfam UK and Ireland's programme in Mexico concentrates on training and supporting local organizations – helping people to defend their interests and improve incomes. In urban areas Oxfam funds training to help people participate in community planning – and legal training for women, often vulnerable and unaware of their rights. Oxfam also promotes networks of groups working with the poor – from farmers to academics – in an effort to influence and propose alternatives that will benefit poor communities.

The publishers would like to thank the following for their help in preparing this book: Larry Boyd, Pauline Martin and Eduardo Klein of Oxfam's Latin American programme; the Ugalde family and the people of La Trinidad; Tracey Hawkins of Oxfam's photo library.

The Oxfam Education Catalogue lists a range of other resources on economically developing countries, including Mexico, and issues of development. These materials are produced by Oxfam, by other agencies, and by Development Education Centres. For a copy of the catalogue contact Oxfam, 274 Banbury Road, Oxford OX2 7DZ, phone (01865) 311311, or your national Oxfam office.

Photographic acknowledgements
The author and publishers wish to acknowledge, with thanks, the following photographic sources:

GSF Picture Library p3. Buzz Mitchell p5 bottom. All other photographs Sean Sprague.

The publishers have made every effort to trace the copyright holders, but if they have inadvertently overlooked any, they will be pleased to make the necessary arrangement at the first opportunity.

Cover photograph: Liba Taylor, Hutchison Library

Note to the reader - In this book there are some words in the text which are printed in **bold** type. This shows that the word is listed in the glossary on page 30. The glossary gives a brief explanation of words which may be new to you.

First published in Great Britain by Heinemann Library, an imprint of Heinemann Publishers (Oxford) Ltd Halley Court, Jordan Hill, Oxford OX2 8EJ

OXFORD LONDON EDINBURGH MADRID ATHENS BOLOGNA PARIS MELBOURNE SYDNEY AUCKLAND SINGAPORE TOKYO IBADAN NAIROBI HARARE GABORONE PORTSMOUTH NH (USA)

© 1996 Heinemann Publishers (Oxford) Ltd.

00 99 98 97 96
10 9 8 7 6 5 4 3 2 1

British Library Cataloguing in Publication Data
Alcraft, Rob
  Mexico. – (Worldfocus Series)
  I. Title II. Sprague, Sean III. Series
  972

ISBN 0 431 07247 7 (Hardback)

ISBN 0 431 07242 6 (Paperback)

Designed and produced by Visual Image
Cover design by Threefold Design
Printed and bound in Britain by Bath Press Colourbooks, Glasgow

A 5% royalty on all copies of this book sold by Heinemann Publishers (Oxford) Ltd will be donated to Oxfam (United Kingdom and Ireland), a registered charity number 202918.